This Little Light of Mine

of Mine

Living the Beatitudes

Kathleen M. Basi

Liguori

ONE LIGUORI DRIVE
LIGUORI MO 63057-9999

Imprimi Potest:
Harry Grile, CSsR, Provincial
Denver Province, The Redemptorists

Published by Liguori Publications
Liguori, Missouri 63057

To order, call 800-325-9521
www.liguori.org

Library of Congress Cataloging-in-Publication Data

Basi, Kathleen M.
  This little light of mine: living the beatitudes / Kathleen M. Basi.—1st ed.
      p. cm.
1. Beatitudes. 2. Families—Religious life. I. Title.
  BT382.B3698 2013
  241.5'3—dc23

                              2012041847

p ISBN 978-0-7648-2223-0
e ISBN 978-0-7648-2288-9

Liguori Publications, a nonprofit corporation, is an apostolate of The Redemptorists. To learn more about The Redemptorists, visit Redemptorists.com.

Printed in the United States of America
17 16 15 14 13 / 5 4 3 2 1
First Edition

Contents

Dedication

A person's faith is a product of everyone he or she has ever encountered. This book, then, can be dedicated to every friend, classmate, teacher, and authority figure who has ever crossed my path. But I would be remiss if I didn't acknowledge my parents, Ted and Therese; my grandmothers, Bernadine and Anna Margaret; and my husband, Christian. Their influence on my journey cannot be overstated.

Introduction

According to a 2009 study done by ARIS (American Religious Identification Survey), the number of people who identify themselves as Christians dropped by eleven percent since 1990. Fully fifteen percent of people—a larger group than any other except Catholics and Baptists—deny any religious belief at all.

If you're reading this book, chances are you're not among the drifters. But chances are that you *do* worry about your children padding the depressing statistics. Raising faithful children has never been a slam-dunk, but in generations past cultural factors put pressure on children as they grew so that even if faith was lukewarm, they would continue to observe the essentials. In a 1940s movie, Bing Crosby played a priest with a heart of gold. Movies, media, and societal norms all upheld the basic goodness of Christianity and took for granted its central place in people's lives.

No longer can we count on that. Nowadays, priests are usually portrayed as pedophiles or tortured souls. Kids are expected to attend sports events not only on Wednesday nights but on Sunday mornings, and virtually the only references to Christianity in the news are those that highlight hypocrisy and scandal.

We wonder how we got to this place. Sexual abuse has something to do with it; so does a simple shift in demographics. Some would blame lackluster religious education, others the sexual revolution.

But in the end, knowing *why* the paradigm has shifted doesn't really change anything. Whatever the cause, the end result is the same, and so is the challenge to parents: to pass on a vibrant faith to our children in the midst of a culture that will undermine our efforts at every turn. What's a parent to do?

It's not enough to teach our children the externals of the faith: the symbols and what they stand for. All that is important, but faith is much more.

Faith is on our minds during the high seasons, as the manger, the cross, and the empty tomb take center stage in all our preparations. But what about the rest of the year? During Ordinary Time, we tend to approach our faith as if it is…well, ordinary. But nearly two-thirds of the year is spent there.

These are the times that make or break a person's faith, the times when we choose to be committed followers of Christ or fall into "PACE" (Palms-Ashes-Christmas-Easter) Catholicism. Is our faith real? Can esoteric, theoretical theology really have an impact on the way we live? How do we answer challenges from both sides of the culture: the one that says faith should be a comfort (in other words, it should never challenge you), or the one that says "since nobody bothers to live it, it's obviously a bunch of baloney?"

I believe our faith can and does answer these questions. But only if we go beyond Sunday mornings, beyond the theory of sacrament and theology, and carry it into Monday business meetings and Tuesday naptimes and Friday date nights. If we're willing to dig beneath the surface, we'll find that our faith can and must be a "feet-on-the-ground" experience, that it calls us to a mission of practical, daily interaction between elevated theology and the mundane tasks of life.

Introduction

Knowing our faith is a great start, but knowledge must lead us to action. John Paul II's groundbreaking series of talks known as the *Theology of the Body* proceeds from a simple concept: Being made in God's image means our actions should reflect God's actions. We are the only beings in the universe who are "souls enfleshed." Angels have souls but no bodies; animals have bodies but no souls. Only humans have both. It is our souls that are made in God's image, but it is with our bodies that we express the love of God; it is through our bodies that we serve him.

Thus, action is the physical manifestation of faith. It is faith made visible, made effective in the world. We must not compartmentalize faith, lock it within safe parameters so that we don't offend or look like religious fruitcakes.

Yet at the same time, Godly action and palpable holiness generally aren't "in your face." Think of those you know who most embody holy living. Often, perhaps most of the time, those whose faith strikes us most forcefully aren't those who talk about it, but those who simply live it—letting the actions speak to the faith that directs them. We all know people who rarely talk about their faith, and yet everyone around them knows it is central to who they are.

When faith becomes a holistic part of our actions, it becomes real, it becomes effective and powerful in the world. That is the goal to which we aspire as Christians, and it is what I hope to help families accomplish in this book.

How to Use This Book

This Little Light of Mine is divided into chapters based on the Eight Beatitudes. Within each chapter, I have broken down other topics of importance to life in faith (for example, the Ten Commandments and the fruits and gifts of the spirit). These are listed in the chapter subtitles.

Each chapter includes sections for adults and children, and ends with a section called "Just Live It." The activities in this section offer you and your family the opportunity to apply the lessons learned to your everyday lives, so that faith becomes integrated into daily living. In some cases, the activities are done as a group. But what is appropriate for a child's level of understanding often doesn't challenge an adult, so in certain cases I have included separate activities for adults and children.

No one can teach well what he or she doesn't know well. The best way to ensure that religious formation "takes" is for parents to live their faith, to be seekers alongside their children. Then, children see that religion is not something you learn about in childhood and consider finished. Rather, it must grow and change throughout life.

For this reason, I've gone into more depth in the sections for adults. I hope these reflections make it easier to synthesize the topics for your children. Use this book as an opportunity to dig deeper, to think about your own faith journey and discern what God is calling you to do. Although I speak to parents, these reflections are for all adults, parents or not, who want a real and active faith, one that lights a fire and spurs you to go out and do something about it. A stagnant faith is a dead faith; my hope is that by using this book, you will find ways to bring your experience of being Catholic out of the theoretical realm and integrate it into real life.

Chapter 1

"Blessed are the poor in spirit, for theirs is the kingdom of heaven" (Matthew 5:3).

First and Second Commandments:
"I am the LORD your God, who brought you out of the land of Egypt, out of the house of slavery. You shall not have other gods beside me. You shall not make for yourself an idol or a likeness of anything in the heavens above or on the earth below or in the waters beneath the earth; you shall not bow down before them or serve them. You shall not invoke the name of the LORD, your God, in vain" (Exodus 20:2–7, excerpts).

Living in Humility

What does it mean to be "poor in spirit?"

I am not God.

This seems like a really obvious truth, but it's one of the hardest lessons we have to learn as human beings. As Christians, we profess to follow God. We pray, "Thy will be done," but every day we have to struggle to act as if we really mean it. That's where Matthew comes in. After all, if I am to be poor in spirit, it must mean I have to do something. But what exactly?

Though difficult most of the time, Jesus' first beatitude calls us to do God's will; to put God and others first; to live humbly. But humility is an uncomfortable garment for most of us, one that takes a lifetime to break in—if we break it in at all. To be humble is to place ourselves—our own desires and concerns— behind those of someone else. To place another first is to place ourselves second.

We're all forced to do this sometimes, when work commitments disrupt our plans, when elderly parents or young children demand more of us than we think we have to give. But for most of us, moments of crisis are not the times when we find it hardest to subordinate ourselves. When things are really tough, we are well in tune with our own smallness, our dependence on God.

No, humility is harder when the daily grind of giving and giving and giving again wears down a willing spirit. When children pass viruses around like candy and a parent hasn't slept for two weeks—when Murphy moves in, and the dishwasher, the car, and the sump pump break in the same week—those are the moments when you cry out, "Enough already! God, just make it stop!" At times like these, it's hard to listen to the still, small voice that whispers, "Darling child, that is your will, but it is not mine." Are we afraid to recognize the humble existence that we have here on earth? Does living in humility allow for these day-to-day moments?

Humility is not tolerating circumstances we can't change while complaining about them through gritted teeth. It is an act of will, a choice to be at peace when our gut reaction is to choke on helpless rage. It means accepting what we don't want to accept, being gracious when we want to complain, and trusting that God has a plan, even if it makes no sense to us.

And at these times, Jesus says, we're blessed?

Well, yes. When Moses' people exploited God, who rescued them from slavery, it didn't take much to make them humble again. And when Jesus calls us to remember God first before ourselves, he calls us to that same humility.

Being poor in spirit, learning to accept humbling circumstances without angst, rescues us from self-righteousness and pride. It's easy to be thankful when I'm on top of the world...at least, for a while. But soon I start thinking that getting my way is no more than what I deserve. I start to forget that everything I have, right down to the very breath of life, is a gift from God. I pay lip service to gratitude, but I act as if I have all the answers. And from there, it's a short step to judging everyone else's circumstances based on my own. In other words, consciously or not, I start to regard myself as God. I become prideful. When I lose focus on God, I regard more earthly things in the same manner as God (see the First and Second Commandments). When all of a sudden I am the main priority in my life (a false god), where is there room for the kingdom of heaven that Jesus promises?

Pride is one of those seven deadly sins, the one that toppled Lucifer and causes all manner of trouble in human relationships. Humility keeps the universe in its proper perspective. Have you ever shaken your fist at heaven and yelled, "What are you *thinking*?"

When God can be understood, it's a sign that we've tried to remake him in our image instead of the other way around. Being poor in spirit means we are able to be at peace with whatever befalls us—a peace that comes only from trusting that God is in charge. Now *that's* a humbling experience (at least, it should be). One who is humble doesn't presume to have all the answers. One who doesn't have all the answers naturally draws closer to

God. This is why the poor in spirit are blessed: because they are, as Matthew said, closer to the kingdom of heaven.

But pride is not the only false god we have to watch out for. These days it's almost cliché to point out how society idolizes things...but that doesn't make it any less true. Debt crises, real estate bubbles, obesity—many of the themes that recur in the news are a symptom of broken humanity caught in the lie that having more will make us happier. The inertia is hard to resist. Our entire economy is built on acquiring more, and everyone suffers when consumption falls off. In such an environment, anything can become an idol: sex, status, food, dieting, exercise—the list is endless.

The thing we have to keep in mind is that all things are good, as long as they are used properly. But the idols we worship end up controlling us. As Matthew says, "You cannot serve God and mammon" (Matthew 6:24).

Regular confession can help us recognize our prideful qualities, in part because a good examination of conscience opens up the mind to recognize our personal idols. But we also have to heed the quiet sense of discomfort such an exercise unearths. Sometimes it's hard to banish those golden calves (Exodus 32) to their appropriate place in our lives. It's as if we are impatient to obtain more and more. The more we anxiously wait, the more we tend to fill our lives with material things.

This is probably why so many saints chose to give away everything they had. When you wear a habit, you don't have to worry about style; when you own nothing, you don't worry about what kind of car makes you look cool. Physical poverty, like crisis moments, makes the most important things in life crystal clear. In fact, the lives of the saints are filled with stories of men and women who sought the most humbling of circumstances in pursuit of holiness. Perhaps the preeminent example for our time is Blessed Teresa of Calcutta. Mother Teresa chose to live among the poorest of the poor in India, ministering to people living in situations so grim that her volunteers frequently became emotionally exhausted.

But few of us are called to that kind of heroism. Most of us live ordinary lives amid family obligations and carpools. While we can strive to emulate Mother Teresa's heart, we might see a more reachable goal in the life of another nun: Saint Thérèse of Lisieux, the "Little Flower of Jesus."

Saint Thérèse dreamed of being a saint, of loving Christ to the fullest extent of her ability. But she was no Joan of Arc. She was a cloistered Carmelite nun, separated from the rest of the world by the walls of her convent. She knew she would never do great deeds; all she could do was small things to the best of her ability. She regarded all her assigned work in the convent—humble tasks like cooking, laundry, and cleaning—as a way to show love for Christ through service.

Thérèse taught us that "ordinary" doesn't mean "unimportant." When we consciously, intentionally dedicate every plebian task to Jesus, the entire tone of a day shifts. Petty irritations become opportunities to empty ourselves, to practice humility.

Family life offers daily opportunities to place others before ourselves. Parents do it instinctively, changing diapers, making meals and cleaning up messes from sunup to sundown. But doing what we must with a sour face is a whole different thing than doing it joyfully, as an act of sacrificial love for Jesus, who resides in our spouses and children. After all, when it comes right down to it, small sacrifices—like not complaining over repeated interruptions or interacting with cranky family members without losing our temper—really aren't small at all. Imagine how life might be transformed if we approach it as Thérèse did!

I'm under no illusions. You will fail every day, just as I failed within twenty minutes of writing these words. But nothing worthwhile is learned overnight, and Christianity is a lifelong journey of discovery.

For the Children

The Eight Beatitudes are full of words we don't really use anywhere else. What does it mean to be "poor in spirit," anyway?

It means we are humble. We can't always have our own way, and that makes us mad sometimes. Have you ever had to miss something special because a brother or sister needed something more? Have you ever felt bad because others got a prize and you didn't? How did you act? Did you whine and complain? Or were you happy for them?

We all have things we want to own or to do—toys, books, places we want to visit, movies we want to see. But it's not all about "me." Being a Christian means we want to do what *God* wants—and sometimes that's not the same thing as what *we* want. Jesus asks us to be happy no matter what happens—even when things don't go our way.

The funny thing is, getting what we want doesn't make us happy anyway. We just start wanting something else instead of being happy with what we have.

To be humble means that even though our life and our desires are very important, everyone else is just as important. It means we can let others get what they want before we do. It means even if we have to go without, we won't be mad about it.

Being humble isn't always an easy thing to do. But I can become better at it if I practice:

- ♥ I can let my sister choose what TV show we're going to watch, even if it's not what I want to watch.
- ♥ I can let my brother have the last piece of pie, even if I have to go without.
- ♥ I can let a friend choose what game we're going to play at recess.
- ♥ I can stop arguing with my classmate, even when I know I'm right.

It sounds hard, doesn't it? But the good news is, the more we practice, the easier it gets!

Just Live It

1. Make a list of the three most important things in your life. Hang it someplace prominent, and every time you want something, look at the list. Does what you want to have or to do support or undermine those priorities?

2. When contemplating a purchase, ask yourself: "Will having this item bring me closer to God, further away, or make no difference?"

3. Think of someone with whom you always seem at loggerheads. Come up with one specific thing you can do to let him have his way—even when you want to claim your own supremacy.

4. Think of a specific act of self-sacrifice or service you can offer to a specific family member, coworker or associate. Write the person's name, the act, or a phrase to remember on a piece of paper. String it around your neck, put it in a billfold or a pocket. For instance, if you are prone to self-righteousness and judgment, you might write, "I do not know anyone's whole story; it is not my place to pass judgment, only to live my life as I believe God is calling me."

Chapter 2

"Blessed are they who mourn, for they will be comforted"
(Matthew 5:4).

"My grace is sufficient for you, for power is made perfect in weakness"
(2 Corinthians 12:9).

Suffering, Freedom, and Sin

Why does God allow suffering?

This is one of the hardest questions we have to answer as followers of Christ. People are always asserting that if there really was such a thing as a loving God, he couldn't possibly allow the horrors that fill our daily newscasts. And let's be honest: We can see their point. The headlines are crammed with violence, hate, and cruelty of all kinds. It's easy to question whether humanity, the crown jewel of creation, really is as "good" as God said (Genesis 1:31).

The culprit, of course, is original sin. We were made to love as God loves: freely, fully, holding nothing back. But such love is a choice; and in a fallen world, it's a choice we fail regularly. We have everything we need for a comfortable life, plus a solid

Christian moral foundation. And yet even with all those benefits, the best of us sin daily. Why should we be surprised that brutality thrives wherever desperation and poverty rule? Let's face it: Cruelty is inevitable in a fallen world.

Still, the answer seems a bit too pat; it leaves out too many disasters. When hurricanes and tornadoes wipe out entire cities, when airplanes crash and diseases ravage, it can shake the foundations of our faith. Supposedly, suffering teaches valuable lessons, but knowing that doesn't help the sufferer. Perhaps one day we'll understand the purpose of it all...but it's just as likely we'll never understand. So why on earth would Jesus say those who suffer are "blessed?"

As Catholics, we believe suffering offered in union with the passion of Christ "acquires a new meaning; it becomes a participation in the saving work of Jesus" (*Catechism of the Catholic Church* 1521). Every Lent, we suffer in communion with Jesus, remembering his sacrifice as we endure our own. In other words, we learn to view our own pain not as something suffered in isolation but as part of a much larger plan. We offer our suffering to God just as we offer our thanks, and it makes the load easier to bear.

At some point, however, almost everyone experiences that inward feeling of isolation, a dark night of the soul, as Saint John of the Cross called it. Some react with faith; and yet others turn their backs on God. What's the difference? An attitude of humility is the strong foundation that allows our faith to weather suffering; fear turns us away. Thus, the first beatitude makes the second possible.

As an example, several years ago, the teenage daughter of one of our parish families died in a car accident. I helped her parents plan the funeral. I remember approaching the meeting with great trepidation, but walking out of it with a sense of awe at the humble faith showed by these people living through every parent's worst nightmare. They didn't understand, but they didn't try to blame God; in fact, God seemed to shine out of the shattered edges of their pain.

Suffering draws us closer to God. At rock bottom, human strength disappears; we can't see a big picture that makes all the agony worthwhile, and so we finally give up and let him take over.

Suffering burns away the banalities that fill up so much of life with chatter and static. It clarifies what really matters. When a child lies in the ICU, you stop worrying about that colleague who's always one-upping you. When a spouse loses a job, having the newest phone doesn't seem terribly important.

My husband and I spent three years trying to conceive before our first child came along. Anyone who has been through infertility knows how punishing a trial it is. You question whether God is getting back at you for (fill in the blank)—and it seems reasonable. You rage at him for opening the wombs of unwed teens. You stop seeing your bodies as the wonder of creation that they are. You lose faith in their ability to do what they were made to do.

At some point in the process, men and women must come to accept that they'll never understand why God asked them to endure this raw, excruciating pain. For us, that moment came when, only weeks before traveling to Russia to adopt, we at last conceived. Why put us through all this, if we were going to have biological children after all?

But we were blessed—doubly so, because eventually, we got to understand why God had asked us to endure that suffering. It happened the day our second child was born and the doctor told us she had Down syndrome. The pain of infertility, we realized, had prepared us for this ultimate lesson in accepting God's will in childbearing.

As unpleasant as it is, suffering is good for us. It stretches the soul, offers opportunities to grow in ways we couldn't without it. And witnessing others' suffering awakens compassion and gives us the chance to demonstrate our love for God, who is present in every human being (Matthew 25:31–45).

Suffering can do all these things, but only if we stop wasting time berating God for mismanaging the universe. When we push aside self and open our hearts to ask, "What lesson do you want me to learn from this?" then we are finally able to participate in God's plan for us.

For the Children

Have you ever wondered why God doesn't stop bad things from happening? There are earthquakes and tornadoes and wars, and people always hurting each other. Why doesn't God make bad guys be good guys?

God created each and every one of us as good people. But he also gave us free will. This means we always have a choice to do the right thing or the wrong thing. He did this because he wanted a family of people who would choose to love, just as he loves. This is what it means to be made "in God's image": not that we look like him, but that we can choose to act like him.

But of course, if we can choose to love, we can also choose not to love. That's what Adam and Eve did when they ate the apple, and it's what we do every time we are unkind to each other. It's called original sin. And when we choose to sin, we cause suffering for others. The more we choose to sin, the more suffering we cause.

There are other kinds of suffering, too. When bad things happen—when someone you love gets very sick or a storm tears up a town—sometimes there's nothing you can do but ask God for help. Second Corinthians says, "My power is made perfect in weakness." We offer our suffering to God the same way Jesus offered his sufferings on the cross. This helps us understand how much our sins hurt God and makes us want to be more like him.

Suffering also helps us remember how much we need God. And when we see other people hurting, it gives us a chance to show God how much we love him. After all, in Matthew 25, Jesus told us whenever we see anyone hungry or thirsty or sick and help them, we're actually helping *him*.

We may never understand why God asked us or someone else we love to go through something bad, but we can learn to trust that he has a plan, even if we can't see what it is.

Just Live It

"In all circumstances give thanks" (1 Thessalonians 5:18).

"Be filled with the Spirit...giving thanks always and for everything in the name of our Lord Jesus Christ to God the Father" (Ephesians 5:18, 20).

Gratitude? In a chapter about suffering? Yes. Gratitude in all circumstances is a brutally difficult lesson to learn, but one that is vital to an authentic Christian life.

Start a "gratitude journal." Buy a notebook or post lists on bedroom doors or in the kitchen. Have every family member record what they are thankful for. In order to cultivate this "attitude of gratitude" in your house, you'll want to establish it as a routine. You might make it a part of bedtime rituals, or if that is a particularly chaotic time, part of family mealtime. Make it work for your family, but be sure it becomes habitual.

Begin by looking for small, ordinary things: the way the sun shines through a potted plant or a breeze blowing through open windows. Encourage your children to be grateful for their favorite "special classes" at school or a sibling's hug upon arriving home.

But don't stop there. Even more important is to exercise gratitude in life's difficult moments. Corrie ten Boom, who was sent to a Nazi concentration camp for hiding Jews during World War II, once told how her sister thanked God for everything, even the flea infestation in their overcrowded barracks. In the end, they found out that the fleas kept the Nazi guards away. Because of this, they were free to host worship services in the barracks.

Look for the silver lining in your reordered priorities and daily frustrations and, if nothing else, thank God for the ways it could have been worse and wasn't. Sometimes the greatest gratitudes are things that didn't happen: the accident narrowly averted, the sick child who didn't have to go to the hospital.

Chapter 3

"Blessed are the meek, for they will inherit the land"
(Matthew 5:5).

"Love is patient. Love is kind....It endures all things"
(1 Corinthians 13:4, 7).

The Gifts and Fruits of the Spirit

The consumer culture is a cliché these days; but like it or not, it tugs on us all. We always want more than we have: more money, a bigger house or car, the newest TV and phone. Acquisition of power, at least over our own destiny, is the goal of almost everything we do, whether or not we realize it. Promotions and a higher salary may help us support our families, but the reality is that we need much less than we want. Have you ever looked at images of third-world poverty and wondered if it's downright immoral to go out for a fancy dinner? Why is that?

If there's one thing you can count on, it's that God will always turn expectations on their head. When the Jews set their sights on a Messiah who would drive the Romans out of Israel, God sent a baby so poor he was born in a manger. When Jesus' disciples expected him to raise a grassroots rebellion, he instead emptied himself on the cross. Why is it that God considers the meek his own special ones?

Maybe it's because they're under no illusions about their own power and importance. When you have nothing, there's no one to depend on but God. Like those who suffer, the meek don't have to work so hard to keep their priorities straight.

We may never be meek in the physical sense of destitution, but we can aspire to separate ourselves from the things of the world and pursue a Godly meekness. Fortunately, the Spirit is waiting to give us what we need. When we admit we are not God (blessed are the poor in spirit), when we learn to weather hardship with grace (blessed are those who mourn), then we become fertile soil, ready to inherit the blessings the Spirit wants to share: the gifts and fruits of the Holy Spirit.

The gifts of the Spirit are wisdom, understanding, counsel, fortitude, knowledge, piety, and fear of the Lord. These gifts are character traits that shape the way we view and interact with the world. These virtues help us recognize God's presence (or absence) in the people, places, and situations we face every day. They help us discern and obey God's will in our lives.

The fruits of the Spirit are charity, joy, peace, patience, kindness, goodness, generosity, gentleness, faithfulness, modesty, self-control, and chastity. These are gifts of another kind: things that others can sense in us through our actions.

The list begins with charity for a good reason. In contemporary usage, this word is associated with giving to the needy, but the Church uses it interchangeably with the word "love." This puts an altogether different spin on it. What we usually call "love," as it is portrayed in movies and songs—a feeling that overwhelms common sense and self-control—is really not love at all. In Godly terms, the definition of love is a series of actions:

> "Love is patient, love is kind. It is not jealous, [love] is not pompous, it is not inflated, it is not rude, it does not seek its own interests, it is not quick-tempered, it does not brood over injury, it does not rejoice over wrongdoing but rejoices with the truth. It bears all things, believes all things, hopes all things, endures all things" (1 Corinthians 13:4–7).

Kindness, goodness, generosity, gentleness, faithfulness—these attributes direct how we interact with others, not only those closest to us, but coworkers, store clerks, and complete strangers. Self-control is key to resisting temptation; modesty and chastity ensure that we treat the temple of the human body (both ours and others') with dignity. Peace is a quality we all would like in greater abundance, but it only comes from within. Patience? Same story.

You can probably think of people you know who embody these qualities. Their faith permeates the world around them. Somehow, they breathe peace into every situation. They don't have to hold up a Bible and call on the name of Jesus; their very presence is evangelization. We can learn from them. Better yet—we can *be* them. Next time you go to the grocery store, ask yourself: When I leave, how will the cashier remember me? Will I leave behind a feeling of patience, kindness, and peace? Remembering the fruits and gifts of the Holy Spirit can help us to embody a Christ-like meekness day to day.

We can also learn from another kind of meekness: age and/or disability. By every measurable standard, my daughter, who has Down syndrome, doesn't make the cut. All the custom orthotics, medical care, and costly education in the world will likely never result in her attaining a high-school reading level. Yet her charisma and zest for life forges bonds wherever she goes. Her very presence in our life has inoculated us from much of the "rat race." She really does seem to have a direct line to heaven. When I think of her, I have no doubt that the meek will, indeed, inherit the land.

For the Children

You know what the amazing part about faith is? Every lesson you learn helps you to be ready to learn the next one. So being humble, like we learned in chapter 1, and learning to be happy even when we suffer, like we learned in chapter 2, gives us what we need to be ready for the third beatitude: Blessed are the meek, for they will inherit the land.

There are some big words in that sentence. To be meek is a lot like being humble. It means we aren't worried about having all the biggest and best clothes and toys. It means we live simply and don't try to be better than everyone else. To inherit means to receive a big gift. Once we've learned to be humble and be happy even when things are hard, we are ready to receive some special blessings the Holy Spirit is waiting to share with us: the fruits and gifts of the Spirit.

The gifts of the Spirit are wisdom, understanding, counsel, fortitude, knowledge, piety, and fear of the Lord. Wisdom and understanding help us know how to recognize what is good in the world. Counsel means knowing how to give good advice. Fortitude means we don't freak out when life gets tough. Piety and fear of the Lord mean that we show God the respect he deserves.

These gifts help us think about God and the world in the right way. And that changes the way we act. The Spirit also gives us

twelve "fruits": charity (also known as love), joy, peace, patience, kindness, goodness, generosity, gentleness, faithfulness, modesty, self-control, and chastity.

Charity is the same word the Church uses to mean "love." Love is more than a good feeling. When God asks us to love, he's talking about the way we treat other people. Saint Paul wrote some famous words about love:

"Love is patient, love is kind. It is not jealous, [love] is not pompous, it is not inflated, it is not rude, it does not seek its own interests, it is not quick-tempered, it does not brood over injury, it does not rejoice over wrongdoing but rejoices with the truth. It bears all things, believes all things, hopes all things, endures all things" (1 Corinthians 13:4–7).

It can be really hard to act with love when we are angry with other people. Many of those other fruits—like kindness, patience, generosity, and gentleness—are ways we can show love to our family members and friends, especially when it's hard. Self-control helps us to treat other people and ourselves with respect, even when we don't want to. That is important because our souls are made in God's image. Since God lives within each one of us, our bodies are holy. Modesty and chastity mean that we respect our bodies and the bodies of everyone around us.

This is too hard for us to do by ourselves. We need God's help. That's why he gives us the gifts and fruits of the Spirit.

Just Live It

1. Make apple dumplings or sugar cookies decorated with the name of a spiritual fruit or gift.

2. Get outside your comfort zone: interact with the powerless. Visit a nursing home or a group home for the disabled or homeless. When we interact with "the least of these," it transforms our outlook on topics related to them, taking our opinions from a theoretical understanding of contemporary issues to one that is powerfully real.

3. Institute a "one in, one out" policy in your household: establish a cap on toys, books, and clothes for both adults and kids in the family.

4. Make a list of needs vs. wants.

5. Place limits on TV, web, phone, game usage—in other words, seek a less "plugged in" lifestyle, since that lends itself to a constant desire for more.

6. Make a mobile. To make a mobile, you will need several horizontal beams, which can be made from a cut-up clothes hangar, twigs, drinking straws or wooden kabob skewers, construction paper and art supplies, hole punch, and string or yarn for hanging.

Mobile

Using the patterns on pages 94 and 95, cut out and decorate **twelve apples (fruits) and seven presents (gifts).** On each one, write "I will share the fruit/gift of _____ by _____."

(*Note*: If you want the mobile to last, you might consider laminating it or coating it with contact paper.)

Punch a hole near the top of each apple or present.

Attach two arms of the mobile to each other by placing them at right angles and wrapping tightly with string on the diagonal, alternating every time. When you are satisfied that they are stable, tie off a long piece of string to use for hanging the mobile. Now you have four "arms." From them you can hang apples, presents, or more horizontal arms. Since there are nineteen items to hang, you'll need multiple levels. You can make more crossed arms, or simply use single horizontal beams. Make the mobile as simple or as complex as you feel capable of balancing.

Assemble the mobile by using string to tie apples and presents to the beams. Remember, balance is a matter of both weight and leverage; you may have to move items toward and away from the center to find the right balance.

Chapter 4

"Blessed are they who hunger and thirst for righteousness,
for they will be satisfied"
(Matthew 5:6).

Third Commandment:
"Remember the sabbath day—keep it holy.
Six days you may labor and do all your work,
but the seventh day is a sabbath of the LORD your God"
(Exodus 20:8–10).

Liturgy and the Liturgical Year

"Remember the sabbath day—keep it holy." What a nice tie-in to the next beatitude: Blessed are they who hunger and thirst. "Hunger and thirst" are two words that draw us, as Catholics, directly to the heart of our faith: the Eucharist.

According to the Vatican II document *Lumen Gentium*, celebration of the Eucharist is the "source and summit" of our faith. In this sacrament, we receive the Real Presence of God, not just into our hearts, but into our physical beings. How can we help manifesting the gift in our daily living? And if we don't keep the Lord's Day holy, how can we hope to live up to our calling at all?

The Liturgical Year

But **Eucharist**, from a Greek word meaning "**thanksgiving**," is more than Communion. We are people of the table and people of the Word, and we explore our liturgical year in cycles. There are two cycles to talk about.

1. Liturgical Reading Cycle. The *Lectionary*, the book that pairs Old Testament to New Testament and links them with psalms, is divided into Sundays, weekdays, and special occasions. Sundays follow a three-year cycle (A, B, C). Weekdays follow a two-year cycle, but the gospel is the same every year; only the first reading changes. Special occasions are things like weddings, funerals, Thanksgiving, social-justice Masses, and so forth.

2. Liturgical Season Cycle. Within this framework, the liturgical year is divided by seasons:

> *Advent:* Color: violet/rose.
> > Length: Four Sundays; the final week is not always a full week.
> > Themes: light, expectation, preparation.

> *Christmas:* Color: white.
> > Length: Ten to fourteen days, lasting until the feast of the Baptism of the Lord.
> > Themes: rejoicing, Incarnation.

> *Lent:* Color: violet.
> > Length: Forty days, but you don't count Sundays, and Lent ends on Wednesday of Holy Week. So if you count Ash Wednesday to Easter inclusively, as most people do, it's actually 46 days.
> > Themes: repentance, preparation for baptism.

Easter: Color: white.
　　　　Length: fifty days.
　　　　Themes: rejoicing, resurrection,
　　　　　　　　freedom from sin.

Ordinary Time: Color: green.
　　　　Length: Thirty-three to thirty-four weeks,
　　　　depending on the layout of the high seasons.
　　　　Ordinary Time begins after Baptism of the
　　　　Lord and is interrupted by Lent and Easter,
　　　　after which it resumes and continues until
　　　　late November, when it concludes with the
　　　　solemnity of Christ the King.

　　　　Theme: There is no "ordinary" time.

No "Ordinary" Time

It's easy to associate "Ordinary Time" with "boring," but nothing could be further from the truth. During the high seasons, we focus in on a portion of the mystery that is God, but during Ordinary Time we celebrate the fullness of the gift. There's nothing *ordinary* about it.

In the introduction to this book I suggested that Ordinary Time is make-or-break time for one's faith. This is when we choose to be committed, feet-on-the-ground Christians, or slide into mediocrity. There is nothing in this beatitude about mediocrity. Despite its obvious eucharistic connections, the fourth beatitude is not about physical hunger or thirst—or even a longing for the Eucharist. The last two words are key: "for righteousness." To hunger and thirst for righteousness is to seek greater understanding and ever-increasing holiness in every moment of life—not just occasionally, not when we have a chance, but all the time. That's a tall order.

The liturgy is our spiritual food, giving us strength and insight to live the Christian life outside the safety of the church walls. The ritual of the liturgy is, by nature, repetitive. It's safe to say everyone zones out more often than we'd care to admit. If you're not paying close attention, it's easy to miss how much of the Mass changes every day.

Liturgical prayers and readings are divided into "ordinaries" (which are the same every day) and "Propers." Most of the assembly's parts are from the ordinary, but the prayers specific to the day—the Propers—break open the Word and connect it with daily life.

The Scripture readings are carefully selected to tie together and underscore a particular message that we need for our life in faith. For example, on the fifteenth Sunday of Ordinary Time, year B, the first reading is Amos 7:12–15. God tells Amos, "Go, prophesy to my people." In the Gospel (Mark 6:7–13), Jesus sends the Twelve out two by two to preach the Good News.

Late in the summer of Year B, we explore the "Bread of Life" discourse from John's Gospel. On the eighteenth Sunday, the *Lectionary* opens with the Israelites grumbling about lack of food in the desert. God responds by sending manna—"bread from heaven." This paves the way for Jesus, who shocks the crowd as he claims, "I am the bread of life; whoever comes to me will never hunger, and whoever believes in me will never thirst." (The quotes are from *Lectionary* 113B.)

Sometimes the threads that bind the readings together are easier to recognize than others. But it's always there. And Scripture isn't confined to the Liturgy of the Word, either. It is woven throughout the Mass. Here are a few quotes you should recognize:

- "The grace of the Lord Jesus Christ and the love of God and the fellowship of the holy Spirit be with all of you" (2 Corinthians 13:13).

- "Glory to God in the highest, and on earth peace to those on whom his favor rests" (Luke 2:14).

- "Holy, holy, holy is the LORD of hosts" (Isaiah 6:3; also echoes Revelation 4:8).

- "Blessed is he who comes in the name of the Lord; hosanna in the highest!" (Matthew 21:9).

The way these prayers and Scriptures are tied together offer us weekly (daily) lessons in Christian living, ones that are meant to help us grow in faith. It's vital, then, that we don't simply show up and go through the motions—rattle off prayers, punch our time card, and get on with real life. We must seek out the intellectual and spiritual food we need and look for the places where "source and summit" meets "wheels on pavement."

Even the ritual words give us those moments. During the consecration at every Mass, for instance, the priest quotes Jesus' words, "Do this in memory of me." But we shouldn't limit the impact of those words to the Eucharist alone. Jesus wasn't just talking about the physical bread and wine they passed around the table. What gives meaning to those simple food items is the suffering, death, and resurrection he bore for each of us.

The night of the Last Supper, Jesus was celebrating Passover. Passover is a yearly memorial of the escape from Egypt. For decades, God's people had been slaves. Not frogs, not grasshoppers, not even water turning to blood would move Pharaoh to release them. So God warned the people of Israel to make preparations for a ritual meal: unleavened bread and a year-old lamb, known as the paschal lamb, whose blood was smeared on the doorposts. The angel of the Lord passed over Egypt that night, slaying every firstborn, both human and beast—except those who had been redeemed by the sacrifice. Pharaoh relented, and Israel crossed the Red Sea in triumph.

Passover pits bondage against freedom, sacrifice against salvation. It's no accident that Jesus' death and resurrection played out against this backdrop. When he broke the Passover bread and passed around the cup, he was tying together the old and the new. He was the paschal lamb, whose blood would redeem the entire world.

This is the pivotal moment in salvation history, and for that reason we remember it every day in the Catholic Church. But familiarity can dull our perception of just how amazing—and terrifying—an act this "remembering" is. After all, if we want to participate fully in the sacrament, we, like Jesus, have to allow ourselves to be broken and poured out for others. For every person, that process looks a little different. As spouses, parents, single or professed religious, our call is different in form, but the same in essentials. The liturgy gives us nuggets to "chew" on a day, a week at a time as we struggle to understand what that call means right here, right now.

What Does That Mean?

Alleluia: derived from the Hebrew word "Hallelujah."
The last syllable is the first two letters of "YHWH" or "JHVH," the name of God. So literally it means "Praise God!"

Amen: literally, "so be it." We think of it as a Hebrew word, but it actually has cousins in Arabic and Aramaic as well.

Hosanna: like "Amen," a word that was used in many ancient languages to express both praise and a plea for salvation.

Kyrie eleison: Greek for "Lord, have mercy." In the early Church, Greek and Latin were both used, and this litany remained after the Mass solidified in Latin.

For the Children

When you hear it's time for church, what's the first thing you think? Do you think, "Oh, no, it's so boring! Why do we have to do this *every week?*"

"Remember the sabbath day—keep it holy," says the Third Commandment. God is reminding us that we need a day to rest and get our focus back where it belongs—on him.

Jesus, too, took time to rest, and in one of his most important speeches, the Eight Beatitudes, he pointed out that when we "hunger and thirst for righteousness," we will get what we ask for.

The celebration of the Eucharist is where we receive what we hunger and thirst for. Through the Eucharist, we receive the Real Presence of God right inside our bodies. How can we help living like Jesus, with that gift inside us?

The Church breaks down the year by seasons and cycles. You may think it's the same thing all the time, but it's not. During Advent, we think ahead to the time when Christ will return. During Christmas, we celebrate him coming to earth to be one of us. During Lent, we remind ourselves how much we need to change to be like God. And at Easter, we praise God for the gift of eternal life.

And then there's Ordinary Time. This long season gets split in half, some of it after Christmas, the rest of it in the summer and fall. During Ordinary Time, we pay attention to what it means to really live out our Christian faith.

Every week, the Scripture readings teach us one important thing about living our faith. For example, one week in the summer, God tells the prophet Amos to go speak his word to the people of Israel. Then, Jesus sends the disciples out to preach the

Gospel. The message? We also have to go out into the world and share the good news!

Even the parts of the Mass that are the same every week have lessons to teach us. During the consecration, the priest uses Jesus' words: "Do this in memory of me." But the thing that made the bread and wine mean something was the fact that Jesus gave his life to save the world. If we really want the Eucharist to mean something in our lives, we have to do what Jesus did—give our lives for others.

That doesn't mean we will be killed. It just means that we have to serve others—to think of other people first, to do things for them even when we don't feel like it. It's hard work, and we need the grace God gives us through going to Mass to help us do it.

Just Live It

Make a habit of talking as a family every week about what you heard in the Sunday readings and prayers. Some families have their kids take notes on the homily; this may not be appropriate for all (or even most) children, but if you have a family member who processes and understands better that way, don't rule it out. Most importantly, ask every person in the family to come up with one or two concrete, measurable things he or she can do to apply the lessons learned at church to their lives in the coming week.

Chapter 5

"Blessed are the merciful, for they will be shown mercy"
(Matthew 5:7).

Fourth through Tenth Commandments:
"Honor your father and mother....You shall not kill.
You shall not commit adultery. You shall not steal.
You shall not bear false witness against your neighbor.
You shall not covet your neighbor's house"
(Exodus 20:12–17).

Putting the Focus on Mercy

When we think about God, we usually focus on his mercy: "He makes his sun rise on the bad and the good, and causes rain to fall on the just and the unjust" (Matthew 5:45) No matter how badly we screw up, God doesn't withhold blessings.

Human beings, on the other hand...that's another story. There's an old truism that says, "What goes around, comes around." People are more likely to repay kindness with kindness and cruelty with cruelty. So we truly are blessed when we fulfill the commandments of the Lord.

In chapter 1, we talked about the First and Second Commandments; in chapter 4, we talked about the Third. The rest of the commandments are where the "rubber meets the road" in terms of living out our faith. They guide us in our relationships with others.

Living out our faith is so much harder in the real world. We have to navigate the tricky line between right and wrong, between righteousness and self-righteousness. The reality is that being Catholic puts us at odds not only with obvious evil, but with virtually all the political and social institutions we consider indispensible. In these commandments we find not only the source of conflict, but also the answer to how to deal with it:

> **Honor your father and your mother, that you may have a long life in the land the LORD your God is giving you.**

At first blush, this commandment seems aimed more toward our children than to us. Most of us learn to appreciate our parents when we have kids of our own. But even so, we never stop butting heads with them. When world views and parenting philosophies clash, we need to treat our parents with respect, for they gave us the gift of life. Call them regularly. Stay in contact and look for ways to defuse tension, even if it means certain topics have to be off limits.

In your parents' waning years, when they might become like children themselves, respect is even more critical. Frustration is inevitable; conflict must be resolved, but it has to be done with a spirit of compassion, kindness, and respect. After all, it has to be hard for a person accustomed to directing his or her own life choices, accustomed to taking care of herself, to slowly lose independence and health. Loneliness is a heavy burden for those whose health traps them at home.

We can also read in this commandment an exhortation to appreciate the wisdom of the generations who came before, even those outside our families.

Just Live It

1. Call your parents once a week for a month, just to chat.
2. Is there a point of conflict in your relationship that you have been sidestepping? Take the time and emotional energy to try to resolve it.

You shall not kill.

The vast majority of us are never going to commit murder. Of course, issues like abortion, euthanasia, and the death penalty lie within this commandment, but really, outside of prolife work, it doesn't seem to have much to do with us.

But there are other ways to do violence to the dignity of the human person. Just think about so-called "reality" TV. So much of it is entertainment, based around people systematically shredding the dignity of others.

No, most of us will never commit homicide, but we all have the capacity to kill another's spirit, to destroy others' reputations. Whether by gossip or by belittling words, we have the power to crush those within our sphere of influence. The way in which we talk to those under our authority, the way we correct their mistakes and their faults has the potential to help them understand and connect with the God who is the ultimate authority—or to alienate them from him altogether, leading to spiritual death. Our behavior is not the only factor—thank God!—but it bears remembering that this, too, is an issue of respecting life.

Respecting the dignity of the human person also means respecting the human body as God created it, in its full, life-giving potential. It means caring for the poor and unjustly treated in the world. It includes caring for the "least of these"—the homeless, mentally ill, and disabled. It means treating everyone with dignity, even people whose choices and beliefs lie utterly at odds with what we believe the gospel calls us to. It has ramifications for the way we talk politics and the way we share our faith. If we respect others' human dignity, we will not make assumptions about anyone's motivations (in other words, pass judgment). We will not belittle them, tell lies or partial-truths about them. We will not reduce them to two-dimensional "bad guys," thinking that the ultimate goal of defeating them or reducing their influence justifies such tactics.

Just Live It

1. How does discipline look in your house (classroom, workplace)? Do you find yourself short-tempered, saying things like, "What's the matter with you? Don't you know...?" How do your children react? What words can you use instead to correct behavior?

2. Does political activism or religious discussion put you in a position where you feel compelled to "trash talk" others in pursuit of a greater good? How can you change that script without compromising your beliefs?

3. What concrete action(s) can you take to uphold or
    support the human dignity of marginalized members
    of society?

You shall not commit adultery.

Adultery is another sin most of us will never commit. But interpreting it at face value takes the easy way out. Faithfulness is more than not cheating. In our marriage vows, we promised to give ourselves fully to each other, holding nothing back, no matter what happens: in good times and in bad, in sickness and in health. "I will love you and honor you all the days of my life." But we don't always honor each other. Sometimes we get busy and, when forced to choose between "me" time and "us" time, we choose self. Sometimes we gripe about our spouses behind their backs instead of doing the heavy lifting of respectful dialogue to work out difficulties.

To live out the vocation of marriage is not just to stick together no matter how bad it gets, growing more and more resentful as irritants pile up and fester. Our calling is to love each other body and soul, to treat each other during times of conflict with the respect we want to receive. There's a terrifying vulnerability in this. What if my spouse doesn't reciprocate? I can't give and give and give, and never receive. But only when we take this risk can we find our way to the true meaning of marital love as God intended it.

Just Live It

1. When you get together with your friends, how do you talk about your spouse? Do chats with friends deteriorate into gripe sessions that leave you more frustrated than you were at the start? Do you speak of your spouse with respect, even when sharing about conflict?

2. How do you and your spouse settle disagreements? Do you strive to see each other's point of view?

3. Institute one or two nights a week devoted solely to couple time. After the kids go to bed, turn off the TV, computer, and phones, and spend time working puzzles, reading together, talking.

You shall not steal.

Much of what was said earlier about "you shall not kill" applies equally to this commandment. In America, we tend to view all time and resources as our own, an inalienable right, jealously guarded from all demands, when really all good things come to us from God and belong to him alone. Whatever we have—gifts, time, talent, treasure—is all meant to be used in his service. Jesus makes this clear in the parable of the talents (Matthew 25:14–30).

That doesn't mean we shouldn't be prudent with our resources. God doesn't ask us to impoverish ourselves physically, mentally, or spiritually. But it does mean we have to be willing to give of ourselves and our bounty to help others, even though we can always think of a dozen ways we'd rather use that time and treasure.

Just Live It

Am I using my time, talents, and treasure to serve God to the best of my ability? Or am I hoarding them away, considering them to be my property? How can I shift that balance in a way I can sustain over time, without exhausting myself and my resources?

You shall not bear false witness against your neighbor.

We've been taught the value of honesty our whole lives. Obviously we shouldn't tell lies that tear down others' reputations—but what about when it's true? Isn't it important to vent our bad feelings to someone? But if we do that, we're tearing down another's reputation, even if, in our view, it's well-deserved.

This is a very dicey subject, because in some situations, we do need to vent. But at the same time, whatever we perceive another's faults and sins to be, we don't know the whole story. It's easy to pass judgment, but we all know what it's like to be on the other side of that dynamic. We have good reasons for our choices; it's unfair for others to think they know better how our life should be lived.

It's important to give people the benefit of the doubt and to assume the best intentions. It's also better to try to work out differences of opinion or philosophy with the people themselves, rather than talk badly about them behind their back. It's not always possible, but when it is, that is the best course of action.

Just Live It

1. Think of someone who rubs you the wrong way, someone you always seem to feel a need to complain about—a boss, a coworker, someone at church, a family member. What is it about that person that makes you feel threatened? Are his words or actions actually interfering with your ability to live out your call? If so, what steps can you take to make it better? If he is not interfering, pray for the grace to keep your thoughts to yourself. You may still need to vent to a spouse or close friend, but in public, be generous in your praise and reserved in censure.

2. The next time you are tempted to pass judgment on someone, try to think of at least two scenarios that would justify, or at least mitigate, that person's choice.

> **You shall not covet your neighbor's house.**
> **You shall not covet your neighbor's wife,**
> **his male or female slave, his ox or donkey,**
> **or anything that belongs to your neighbor.**

Oh, this is a tough one. Jealousy is one of those universal human weaknesses. The world is full of good and enjoyable things. No matter how much we have, there will always be something more we'd love to acquire. We can be jealous of others' good fortune, their happiness in marriage, their beautiful family or their children's accomplishments in sports or arts or academics.

Jealousy is inevitable. The question is, how do we act on it? It's important to counter jealousy with an honest look at our own lives, at the blessings we take so much for granted. Then we don't even notice what we were jealous about anymore.

Just Live It

1. Put a rein on the Green Monster. Think of five things you wish were different about your life, things you see others enjoying in their lives. Now, think of ten things about your life that others envy and say a prayer of thanks for them.

2. Set priorities and exercise self-control in spending. In America, we're constantly urged to buy, buy, buy. Consumption drives our economy. But the expectation that we must always have the newest and "best" drives many people into debt. Take a hard look at your life. Are you living within your means? Are you able to give to the Church and/or charities? Are you able to save for your future? If the answer to these questions is "no," maybe it's time to exercise the fruit of the Spirit—self-control—and have the courage to set priorities that are out of line with the cultural norm.

For the Children

Have you ever heard that old saying, "What goes around, comes around?" That's kind of what Jesus is getting at here. God is good to everyone all the time, but people have trouble being nice to those who are mean to them.

The last seven of the Ten Commandments tell us how we should treat other people. Here are some things to think about:

Honor your father and your mother.

Jesus told us to call God our Father. God knows what it feels like to love children and want the best for them. He also knows what it feels like when his children hurt themselves because they didn't do as he said.

Your parents aren't perfect like God is. They make mistakes, just like you do. And yet, just like God, they keep loving you and taking care of you no matter what. God wants you to appreciate your parents and respect them for what they do, the same way you love and respect him.

Just Live It

Think of one little thing you can do for your parents every day this week. Can you clear the table or take the trash out without being asked? Can you help wash dishes or fold clothes? Can you follow directions without complaining?

Whatever you choose, offer that one thing up to God with a little prayer of thanks for your parents and everything they do for you.

You shall not kill.

Most of us are never going to kill anyone, but that doesn't mean this commandment is an easy one to follow. There are people we just don't like, and sometimes we say mean things to or about them. "I don't like playing with you." "You're not very good at sports." "I'm a better reader than you."

The way we talk to other people and what we say about them when they aren't around can make them feel that they are important and loved, or it can make them feel like they are worthless. When we hurt other people's feelings, we are "killing" their spirit. God wants us to talk about other people with respect and not trash their reputation.

Has anyone ever said something to you that made you feel useless? Have you ever said something like that? The next time you're frustrated or hurt, before you speak, think about what words you are going to use.

Just Live It

How can you tell people they hurt you without doing the same thing to them?

You shall not commit adultery.

Adultery is when married people break their promise to be faithful to their spouse. Some day you might be married, too, so for now, practice being faithful to your friends and family members. When you talk about them, be sure you only say things you wouldn't mind them hearing.

You shall not steal.

Sometimes we think we have the right to have whatever we want, just because we want it—no matter who has it. Have you ever taken a toy or book from a sister, a brother, or a friend? How do you feel when someone takes something that belongs to you?

In our world, there are many people who have almost nothing. But most of us have much more than we need. We aren't stealing from others, but sometimes we act as if we have a right to go buy whatever we want. But we are supposed to use everything we have to serve God. People in countries like America use up a lot more food and resources than in other parts of the world, and a lot of it goes to waste. That's not serving God. Do we really need everything we think we need? Can we use a little less and send the extra to someone who is going without?

Just Live It

Do you have clothes or toys that you can give to someone in need? Try to spend less time with your toys and let someone else have a longer turn (you might realize how little you really need the toy!)

You shall not bear false witness against your neighbor.

In other words, don't lie—about anything, but especially about other people.

Sometimes it seems like it's easier to lie. You know you're going to get in trouble if you tell the truth. As long as nobody finds out, a lie will keep you out of trouble. Right?

That's not what God wants, though. Lies eat us up inside. Sometimes they hurt us. And sometimes they hurt other people. We should never tell lies about other people. But sometimes, even saying something that's true about a person can hurt them. Sometimes we don't understand why people act a certain way, why they do things we don't agree with. We assume that they are bad people, but most of the time, they aren't. At times like those, the best thing to do is usually just not to say anything at all.

Just Live It

How could you change your words so that you aren't hurting someone? What can you say to help someone that might be hurting another person?

> You shall not covet your neighbor's house. You shall not covet your neighbor's wife, his male or female slave, his ox or donkey, or anything that belongs to your neighbor.

Covet means to want what someone else has for yourself. Your friend gets a new video game, and suddenly yours looks boring. The most popular girl in the class walks in wearing a new dress, and suddenly you think all your clothes are ugly and out of style. Your best friend gets to go on an awesome vacation, and you want to hide in the trunk and go along.

It's not like you want to go over and steal the video game or take the dress away. It's just that you want one, too!

This world is full of beautiful and fun things, and there's nothing wrong with enjoying them. The trouble comes when having what everybody else has becomes the most important thing in your life. Lots of people have bought things they can't afford and don't need. Then they wonder why they're not happy. You'll never have "enough"—there will always be something else you want. That's because things never really make us happy. Only God can do that.

Just Live It

Make a list of the things you want that you don't have. Now make another list of the things you *do* have that you forgot about.

Chapter 6

"Blessed are the clean of heart, for they will see God"
(Matthew 5:8).

Sacraments and Private Devotion

Most of us spend our whole lives searching for the meaning of life. Every time we think we get close to an answer, something knocks us off course again. We hunger and thirst for—what? All we really know is we're incomplete, and nothing we pursue quite fills the emptiness, because it's God we ache for, God we need. But God can feel far away at times; and the journey to reach him long and uncertain. Along that road, we need sustenance: tangible, physical touch points to strengthen us on the way. We find that sustenance in the sacraments and in a rich heritage of private devotions.

The Sacraments

The sacraments provide sustenance for the Christian journey. Some, like baptism, can only be received once. Others, like Communion and reconciliation, are meant to be received regularly—the more often, the better.

Sacraments, by definition, are outward (that is, physical) signs that reveal an inner (that is, spiritual) grace. We are souls enfleshed, and as such, we have a unique place in the universe. Animals have bodies but not souls; angels have souls but not bodies. Among created beings, only humans have both. Our purpose in God's plan is to manifest his love in the physical world. So the sacraments that give us strength for this task are also a combination of the tactile and the spiritual.

Baptism

Baptism is the first, the basic sacrament, the one that makes us part of the family of God. It erases the effects of original sin and as such it is the first sacrament of forgiveness.

Physical symbols:

Water symbolizes cleansing from sin.

Oil was used to anoint God's chosen one. It symbolizes our call to be "priest, prophet, and king."

The white garment represents being "clothed in Christ," a reminder that we are to keep our Christian dignity unstained until we go out to meet Christ at his Second Coming.

Light represents Christ; we are to keep the flame of
   Christ's light alive in our (and our children's) hearts.

Just Live It

Most children have no memory of their special day. If you have a baby doll in the house, use it to show your children how the physical symbols of baptism were used on them; for example: "When you were baptized, your godparents, your father (mother) and I laid our hands on you, like this." (Have your children lay hands on the doll.) "Then the priest poured water and said, '(name), I baptize you in the name of the Father, and of the Son, and of the Holy Spirit.'" Continue through the other symbols, using your child's baptismal garment and/or candle, if you have them. Another fun activity would be to watch a home video of your children's baptisms, if you have them.

Reconciliation

On the evening of the resurrection, Jesus appeared to the Apostles. He "breathed on them and said to them, 'Receive the holy Spirit. Whose sins you forgive are forgiven them, and whose sins you retain are retained'" (John 20:22–23). Thus was the sacrament of penance born.

Confession is uncomfortable for many of us. Although we know we're receiving the grace of forgiveness, we don't always feel like anything earth-shattering has happened, and we're a nation of people who want, first and foremost, to feel.

But forgiveness doesn't require us to feel it. It only requires that we truly regret our sins and want to leave them in the past as we follow Christ into the future. God does the rest. Our job is to invest the time and energy to pray our way through a good examination of conscience and to enter the confessional with hearts engaged: truly contrite, open to hear God's quiet voice and act on it.

And really, that's hard enough. Facing the mirror and being honest about the blemishes we see is no fun; still less so is bringing those sins to light, even in the privacy of the confessional. Actually, we're only required to receive the sacrament for grave or mortal sins. For minor sins, the habitual ones we commit every day, we can confess directly to God. But that's the easy way out. Most of us don't commit mortal sins often (if at all). Habitual sins, however, have us chained tightly; they can be excruciating to excise. We need the grace of the sacrament on them.

Part of being reconciled is repairing the damage done to relationships by sin. For that, we have to go to the person (or people) against whom we sinned. This requires humility and a healthy dose of meekness (remember those beatitudes?). It's far easier to let conflicts retreat into the background, where we can pretend they never happened, instead of apologizing and making amends. In marriages, this can easily lead to simmering resentment. In children's relationships, the damage is less lasting, but the pliable, soft heart of childhood eventually gives way to the grudge-holding heart of an adult. In both cases, the hard work of self-emptying required on both sides of an apology—because we all know offering forgiveness and showing mercy is at least as hard as expressing sincere regret—can only help everyone involved. This week, slow down and take time to resolve conflicts instead of sweeping them under the rug.

Physical symbols:

The **priest** represents the person of Christ, who offers forgiveness to the contrite.

Absolution is given by a physical **sign of the cross**, traced over the penitent.

Just Live It

Go to confession as a family. Have younger children do a simple examination of conscience while parents and older siblings receive the sacrament.

Eucharist

We dug into the sacrament of the Eucharist in depth in chapter 4. We should never take this sacrament for granted, as something to which we're entitled. In some parts of the world, people regard the Eucharist with such devotion that they will only receive it when they feel they've confessed properly. For this reason, many people don't go at all. That's not God's idea of how this is supposed to work. Confess regularly and approach Communion with the awe and reverence due the presence of God in our midst.

Physical symbols:

Bread and **wine**, which become the Body and Blood of Christ.

Just Live It

Try celebrating a Passover meal with your family. Look up the traditional foods online, or keep it simple, with lamb and a loaf of unleavened bread. Unlike bread for Mass, it doesn't have to consist solely of wheat flour and water.

Recipe (from food.com):

4 cups whole-wheat flour
1 cup white flour
2 cups water
1/4 cup honey
1 1/2 teaspoons salt
1/4 cup oil

Directions:

1. Roll out to 1/8-inch thick.
2. Place on greased cookie sheet.
3. Score into about 1-inch squares.
4. Cut into 4-by-5 rectangles.
5. Bake at 400 degrees about 15 minutes.
6. In the first minutes of baking, prick bubbles that may form.

(http://www.food.com/recipe/unleavened-bread-for-passover-134022)

During the meal, ask all in attendance to think about what it is they need Jesus to deliver them from. What is the habitual sin that you can't overcome on your own? As you pass the bread around the table, have all people break off a piece to eat, and if they feel comfortable, share their thoughts aloud. But don't force it. Conversion happens inside and manifests outside in different ways for different people. It would be easy for an exercise like this to turn into an opportunity to be self-righteous, which defeats the whole purpose.

Confirmation

Confirmation is one of the sacraments of initiation, along with baptism and Eucharist. In the early Church, the sacraments were received together, at Easter, with the reception of the Eucharist as the pinnacle of initiation into the community.

Today, adults entering the Church follow this same pattern, but for children born into Catholic families, the picture is different, and confirmation is the final sacrament received. It consists of an anointing with chrism and the laying on of hands. But although chrism is used to anoint the newly baptized child, too, confirmation is not mere repetition of something done years before. According to the catechism, "The faithful are born anew by Baptism, strengthened by the sacrament of Confirmation" (*CCC* 1212). It is a completion of the grace first experienced in baptism, and with it, the faithful person receives the Holy Spirit, who gives us the gifts and fruits we need to live a faithful life.

Physical symbols:

Chrism oil, **laying on of hands**.

Just Live It

Traditionally, a candidate for confirmation chose a new name, a saint he or she wanted to pattern his or her life after. Although not everyone chooses a new name these days, it can be a great way to help you envision what you want your life in Christ to look like. If you were being confirmed today, who would you choose as a saint, and why? What about his or her life would you try to emulate—and how can you start making it real in your life today?

Holy Orders

Vocations are a hot topic in the Church today. Everyone knows we need more of them—everyone has a culprit they want to blame for the lack of them. But many have pointed out that it's not a crisis of vocations we have today, but a crisis of response. God is still calling, as he has through the ages; the question is, do we teach our children to listen?

Most Catholics pay lip service to encouraging vocations, but when it comes to our own children, we tend to shy away from the subject. It can feel artificial to encourage our kids to consider the priesthood or religious life. We don't want them to feel like we're pressuring them to become priests (or sisters, nuns or brothers, who are not ordained and thus do not receive the sacrament of holy orders). The trouble is, we do talk to them about marriage. Have you ever said, "Some day when you get married..." or, "Some day you'll have kids...?" The way we approach these topics—talking about one as inevitable while shying away from the other—sets up the understanding that marriage is normal, and religious life is weird.

Every person is called to a life's vocation by God, and none are less important than the others. Ask any priest, seminarian, or sister how to encourage vocations and they will tell you to begin by modeling a fully lived vocation of marriage for the children to see. It's time to end the taboo and bring all vocations to the table. Otherwise we are placing barriers in the way of our children discerning what exactly God has in mind for them.

Happiness in life can only be found when a person follows the call of God, whatever form that takes. We should never try to push our children toward one vocation or another, but look for opportunities to get them thinking about the priesthood or religious life as well as marriage. It may feel forced to you, but so do many other important topics—conversations about drugs, alcohol, and sex, for instance. Especially in the young years, children are sponges, soaking up their parents' attitudes based on what they are told—and what they are not told. They tend to take things in stride that adults agonize over.

Physical symbols:

Oil of the catechumens is used to anoint the new priest's hands, symbolizing the power to consecrate.

The **white garment** symbolizes the priest becoming the person of Christ.

Just Live It

Have a priest and/or consecrated religious person over for dinner and find out what their life is really like. Better yet, make this a regular practice and make friends with a priest and/or religious (or several!).

Marriage (Holy Matrimony)

Marriage seems such a given in modern life, we sometimes lose sight of how radical an idea God is calling us to in this vocation. This isn't about falling in love, donning a beautiful dress and living happily ever after; it's a choice to give oneself completely to another, just as Christ gave up his life for the Church (Ephesians 5:32). Nothing may be withheld, if we are to mirror the love of God. There is no "mine" and "yours," and there is no exit strategy. If we want our marriages to honor God, it's an all-in commitment, and only with divine help is it even possible.

Physical symbols:

Though we most often think of rings and a white dress as symbols of marriage, neither of those is essential to the sacrament. What is essential is the physical union of two becoming one (the vows). The marriage act is where the vows, which promise a complete self-gift, become real. This is why the Church teaches that all sexual acts must be open to the possibility of life, for how can couples claim to give and receive each other fully when such a major part of who they are is off-limits to each other and to God? The Church's least-popular teaching simply acknowledges what human beings were created to be. We are most ourselves when we use our bodies in harmony with the way God created them. Through marriage, we become one; and as one, we look to the future of the possibility of life (openly and honestly).

Just Live It

Have an "anniversary dinner" as a family. Look at the wedding album and/or video, make a cake, and share with your children the many ways in which you blended your two lives into one—traditions, ways of running a house. Also celebrate the ways in which your children are a blending of your families: physical resemblances, habits, likes/dislikes, and so on. For those with adopted children, talk about the adoption process and the way you melded the child's pre-existing routines with those of your family.

Anointing of the Sick

Nobody likes to think about getting sick. Even less do we like thinking about death. And yet both of those experiences are universal in human life. This sacrament reminds us to offer our sufferings in union with Christ's passion. When we do, pain takes on "a new meaning; it becomes a participation in the saving work of Jesus" (*CCC* 1521). It may be received by anyone suffering from significant illness or an ongoing medical condition, but it is most commonly thought of for those approaching death. When celebrated along with penance and reception of the Eucharist, anointing is part of the Church's Viaticum, or "last rites." It is meant to give comfort, peace, and courage for the last part of the human journey.

Physical symbols:
The oil of the sick.

Just Live It

Call the church office (or check the bulletin) to find out names of parishioners who are in the hospital or shut-ins. Make cards, spiritual bouquets, or paper flower bouquets and send them, or better yet, hand-deliver them and visit.

Devotions

In addition to the sacraments, the Catholic Church has a rich heritage of personal devotions that are not part of the official liturgy of the Church but which the faithful are encouraged to use as a way to incorporate faith into all parts of daily life. Here is a small sample:

✝ Adoration of the Blessed Sacrament

✝ Rosary

✝ Divine Mercy Chaplet

✝ Novenas—by definition, nine days' repetition of a single prayer in honor of a saint or particular occasion

✝ Wearing a scapular

✝ Wearing saints' medal

✝ Stations of the Cross

✝ Intercessory prayer through the saints (see chapter 7)

Each of these opportunities for prayer has the power to shape us and sustain us on our Christian journey. In popular songs and press, we sometimes hear people talk about "answered" versus "unanswered" prayers—as if a prayer is only answered if we get what we asked for. In Catholic culture, it comes in the form of little "novenas never known to fail," left in church like pious chain letters.

But prayer is not about telling God what to do. Prayer is about opening our hearts and allowing God to change us, to align us with his will and mold us in his image. It is a good and holy thing to ask God for healing, for rain, for whatever we think we need or want—but the part we often leave out is the all-important tag line: "Not my will but yours be done." (Luke 22:42) Whatever form our personal prayer takes, it should point us toward God, and God's will alone.

Just Live It

Do some Internet research and find a devotion that seems to apply to the circumstances of your family and your life. Can you incorporate it into your family prayer?

For the Children

Doing the right thing always makes you feel better after you do it, but sometimes it's hard to do in the first place! We need God's grace to make us strong enough to follow him. But how do you touch God to receive his grace? The sacraments are special ceremonies that use physical symbols to help us feel God's presence.

In *baptism,* we are born into God's family. During baptism, we use:

Water to show that our sin is washed away.

Chrism oil to anoint us, just like kings and prophets have always been anointed when they were called to serve God.

A white garment to symbolize being clothed in Christ.

Light to show that Christ, the Light of the World, lives within us.

Reconciliation, or *penance*, is when we go to the priest and confess our sins.

The **priest** represents Christ, who offers forgiveness to us if we are sorry for our sins.

"**Absolution**" is when the priest tells us our sins are forgiven. As he speaks the words, he traces the sign of the cross over us.

Eucharist is when we receive Communion. Whenever we eat and drink, we remember that, just like Jesus, we are called to give our lives to others.

> During the Eucharistic Prayer, the **bread** and **wine** become the Body and Blood of Christ.

At *confirmation*, we are "sealed" in the Holy Spirit. Long ago, kings used to fasten their letters with a "seal" to give it authority. When people saw their mark on the paper, they knew it was the real thing. Today, governments and other organizations still do this. To be sealed in the Holy Spirit means the Spirit has claimed us for himself and lives within us.

> **Chrism oil** is used as a symbol of the Spirit.

> The bishop (or sometimes the priest) **lays his hands** on our forehead to pray a blessing.

Holy orders is the sacrament in which men become priests or deacons. Sisters, nuns, and brothers profess religious vows, but they are not ordained. But we like to talk about all these forms of religious life together because they are a special calling from God to serve his people in an extraordinary way. God has a plan for each one of us. For some, it means being ordained a priest or professing religious vows. For others, it means being married and raising children. God even calls some people to stay single. But the important part is to ask God what he has in mind for you, and to listen so you know what he wants.

Symbols of Holy Orders:

Oil of the catechumens is used to anoint the priest's hands, showing that he can now consecrate the bread and wine at Mass.

The white garment symbolizes the priest becoming the person of Christ.

Marriage is more than a wedding. Those who are called to marriage are called to give themselves completely to each other—to hold nothing back from each other.

In marriage, man and woman want to be close to each other, and that closeness is how God binds them together and brings children into the world.

Anointing of the sick is a sacrament for people who are very ill or who have a medical condition that causes them to suffer all the time. It is especially important when a person gets close to dying.

The oil of the sick is used to anoint the person and help him offer his suffering to Jesus, who suffered on the cross.

Chapter 7

"Blessed are the peacemakers, for they will be called children of God" (Matthew 5:9).

Celebrating the Saints

Devotion to the saints is one of the things that sets Catholics apart from many other Christian denominations. It's also one of the most misunderstood. Even Catholics often say we pray "to" the saints: Pray to Saint Anthony—he'll help you find your keys. But the Ten Commandments are quite clear: there is only one God, and praying to anyone else is idolatry. It's important to think about the relationship we have with saints and that praying *to* them is really praying *with* them.

Our relationship with the saints is much like our relationship with the people we talk to every day: We ask them to pray for us. Together we make up a community of believers that exists independent of time, distance, and even death. No matter what happens to the body, the soul—the part of us made in God's image—lives forever. The living and the dead are bound together in Christ's mystical body. This is called the communion of saints.

If the living and dead are bound together, then we can pray

for those who have died and call on them to pray for us. At the beginning of November, we celebrate two feasts back to back. All Saints Day celebrates those who have died in Christ, whether formally recognized by the Church or not; All Souls Day is a day of prayer for everyone who has died, regardless of the state of their soul.

Living in community with those who have walked the same path we tread is a powerful thing. It helps to know we're not alone, that others know what we're going through. And their example can help us on our own journey. That, at its core, is the purpose and the value of devotion to the saints.

But let's go back to the community of saints. It is important to distinguish, for example, our dead relatives from Mother Teresa. There are two kinds of saints: little "s" and big "S." The process of becoming an official, recognized saint (big "S") is meant to be long and involved, although it can be shortened and has been several times in recent memory.

After the death of a person known to be holy, an extensive investigation is performed. Have there been any miracles attributed to this person's intercession? Are his or her writings or words faithful to doctrine? Was he or she martyred? Only after the Church is sure the candidate is the real deal—including a verified miracle—is he or she "beatified." Then another miracle and more investigation is required before a person is officially declared a saint, with a feast day included in the canon of saints (hence, the word canonization).

Since every age and nation has produced faithful men and women, the list is always growing. Many of the saints left behind writings, visions, and other aids to the faithful. Saint Thérèse Lisieux, for instance, left the Little Way. Saint John Climacus left us the ladder of divine ascent; Saint Faustina, the Divine Mercy chaplet. We can use these to help us on our Christian journey.

Studying the lives of the saints can inspire us to holier living. When we learn about their passions, struggles, and insights, we discover that they faced many of the same problems we do. Just having proof that someone managed to live an outstanding life is a point of hope. And maybe—just maybe—their solutions can become ours.

For the Children

Even though our bodies die, our souls live forever. That means we can still pray for people after they've left the earth—and they can still pray for us. That's what we mean when we talk about the "communion of saints." (Do you remember that phrase from the Creed we pray on Sundays?)

This is why we talk to the saints—we're asking them to pray for us. On November 1 and 2 every year, we celebrate two feasts. All Saints Day is for saints—in other words, people who lived holy lives and are now with God. All Souls Day is the day we remember everyone who has died, whether or not they are in heaven.

Different saints are known as "patrons" of certain things because of the way they lived their lives. Saint Valentine, for instance, became patron of lovers because he helped Christian couples get married when they were being persecuted in ancient Rome. Learning about the saints helps us understand what other Christians did to stay faithful when they came up against the same kinds of problems we face.

Do you have a patron saint? What do you know about him or her?

Just Live It

1. Halloween originated as All Hallows Eve—the vigil of All Saints Day. Dressing up originally meant dressing up as a saint. This year, reclaim that tradition. Have everyone in the family research a saint and come up with three to five important points in his or her life. Then dress up as that saint for Halloween. Most importantly, come up with one specific thing from his or her life that you can incorporate into yours.

2. Choose a patron saint for your family—someone you admire, whose work you would like to continue. Keep in mind that whatever you do, it has to be able to weave into the fabric of ball practices, music lessons, and other commitments. Do some digging. Find out about the person—what he was known for; what her background was. Then think creatively about how to celebrate the feast day and—even more importantly—how to incorporate the saint's example.

Here are some ideas:

Saint Francis (October 4) was known for a love of animals and God's creation. Visit the humane society or the zoo for a fun activity, or choose a park or drainage creek to clean up.

Saint Maximilian Mary Kolbe (August 14) believed religious indifference was a huge threat and spent his priesthood combating it. He was sent to Auschwitz, where he took the place of a man sentenced to die by starvation as punishment for another prisoner's escape. Honor him by coming up with one concrete practice you can incorporate to live the faith more fully (think Lenten practice, only make it permanent) or by learning about the people who suffered and died during the Holocaust. You can do this online or by visiting a Holocaust memorial or museum (there are several around the country).

Saint Catherine of Siena (April 30) cut off her hair to convince her mother she didn't want to get married. She spent her adulthood serving the ill and the poor and acting as emissary between medieval rulers and the pope. Perhaps several members of your family can donate hair to a charity that makes wigs for cancer patients. For a more ongoing observance, set up a regular time to take care packages to local hospitals.

The possibilities are endless. How can family members incorporate the Little Way into their interactions with classmates and coworkers? Can you emulate Mother Teresa's service of the "least of these" by sponsoring a child or cooking for a food pantry once a month? Can you honor Saint Gianna by volunteering at the crisis pregnancy center?

Keep in mind that simple things can often make the biggest difference. Mow an elderly neighbor's lawn. Bring meals to new parents, not just within your parish, but in your neighborhood and larger community. In my hometown, a local music teacher has her graduating seniors do a recital as a benefit for a local charity.

You can also use mealtime to incorporate the feast. The website Catholic Cuisine (http://catholiccuisine.blogspot.com/) offers meal planning with a Catholic twist.

Chapter 8

"Blessed are they who are persecuted for the sake
of righteousness, for theirs is the kingdom of heaven.
Blessed are you when they insult you and persecute you and
utter every kind of evil against you [falsely] because of me"
(Matthew 5:10–11).

Persecution in the Modern World

The thing about faith in the modern world is that it seems so much harder than it was in the Bible. God doesn't come down and speak out of a burning bush anymore; we don't have long conversations in which we hear a voice speaking words we can't mistake, telling us exactly where to go, and when to go there, and what to do along the way. Nowadays, it all requires so much...faith.

In other ways, though, it seems too easy. What do we really have to struggle against, after all? When we hear about saints offering to take the place of a man condemned to death, or facing the lion pits of ancient Rome, it's hard to take our own obstacles seriously. Don't you ever wonder how you would react if someone held a gun to your head and asked you to deny Christ? Do you ever wonder if you'd have the courage to stand up for your faith, if your life—or worse, the life of one you love—was on the line?

This beatitude seems as far from our day-to-day life as it is possible to be. At least for those of us in the First World, persecution is a thing of the past.

Isn't it?

There are places in the world where persecution of Christians is alive and well in its classic sense—the threat of death, torture or imprisonment for belief in Christ. But for most of us, persecution takes the form of mockery, derision, or contempt. We feel compelled to downplay our faith in order to be taken seriously. People may claim that our faith isn't real because we've never rebelled against it, never tested it and returned. When discipleship leads us to life practices that others find threatening or strange, like using natural family planning or living simply and less luxuriously than the norm, people may roll their eyes and call us out of touch with the real world, or make any number of other belittling, contemptuous remarks.

Does that sound too ordinary to be persecution? Let's take it a step further, then. If you are open about being a Catholic, people will try to make you answer for sexual abuse scandals and the Spanish Inquisition. They'll call the Church corrupt because of the wealth of art and jewels given to it over the centuries and act as if you are responsible somehow. Certain Christians might even manifest anti-Catholicism in their treatment of you.

And sooner or later, if your striving to live a faithful life permeates all your actions, someone will try to corrupt you. It's human nature to tear people off their pedestals. In the teen years, peer pressure can take on this dimension. I remember several times when high school and college associates tried to corrupt me specifically because I was known as that goody two-shoes Catholic girl. In adulthood, it might be more insidious, but it's still there.

All this may seem trivial when compared to being burned at the stake, shot by firing squad, or thrown to lions. Yet these kinds of persecution are equally real, and perhaps, in some ways, even more dangerous. At least when it's life and death, the choice is stark and uncomplicated. Little persecutions tempt us to bury our faith, to compartmentalize it, to keep it private. And we might not even realize it's happened, because we're still going to church and praying and observing all the right externals. But faith without works is impotent, and after all, isn't that the purpose of persecution—to undermine the power of faith?

Once again, the beatitudes paint Christian life in contrasting colors. The eighth beatitude tells us we are blessed when we're not comfortable. Complacency leads to self-satisfaction, and self-satisfaction to self-righteousness, which sets up self as a false god. Trials and tribulations lay before us a choice: to be real, and live what we say we believe, or to sink into mediocrity. Being challenged in our faith may not be comfortable, but faith isn't supposed to be comfortable.

The gospel is inherently antagonistic toward the world. Jesus made that pretty clear when he said, "If the world hates you, realize that it hated me first. If you belonged to the world, the world would love its own; but because you do not belong to the world, and I have chosen you out of the world, the world hates you" (John 15:18–19).

Modern America has a strong Christian presence, but it's more a cultural than a true Christianity. Faith is trotted out in election years by every politician; pundits raise the Christian "flag" every time someone says "happy holidays" instead of "Merry Christmas." But really, are these the things a disciple of Christ should be spending time on? Governments are huge and hard to move in the direction of the gospel, no matter what faith or philosophy its leaders hold, and the word "holiday" is nothing more than a derivation of "holy day." All these petty squabbles distract us from the challenge issued by the gospel, and make no mistake, the gospel does issue a challenge (many of them, in fact, and all of them opposed to human wisdom): If you have two coats, give one away. (Really? Shouldn't I at least have a nice coat for church and work and one for every day?) Sell all you have and give it to the poor. (Are you serious? How am I supposed to survive, let alone take care of my family? I don't want to be a burden on others!) Forgive seventy times seven times. (Now, that's just unhealthy! You have to protect yourself from that kind of abuse and leave the relationship!)

Authentic Christian living will always be threatening. How can it not? If our insides twinge at the thought, how do we expect others to react?

We've spent eight chapters now turning the human view of "blessing" upside down. It seems fitting to end with the hardest one of all. What Jesus is asking us to accept is that joy is not dependent on good things happening to us. Everything is a blessing when it draws us closer to him. Even the darkest parts of our lives are occasions for gratitude, for recognizing that life itself, however difficult or pain-filled, is a blessing simply because it gives us the chance to learn to love God more...but only if we choose to pursue the opportunity.

Just Live It

(**Note**: *this "Just Live It" is way over a child's head. See the next section for an action item for children.*)

Have you ever been singled out for criticism or made the butt of a joke because of your faith? Have you ever not asked off work to go to holy day Mass because you were afraid your boss would think you were a religious nut? Were you deliberately held back when you had an opportunity to witness, for fear of being judged pushy?

In any instance of persecution, being caught unprepared makes it even more difficult to remain faithful to Christ. Do some soul searching. What aspects of your life and habits are most likely to attract the world's contempt? Ask the Holy Spirit to guide you in finding the right words—the ones that will resonate and witness, instead of widening the gap between you and the other person. Perhaps there aren't any words. How, then, do you respond in a Christ-like way—respecting the God-given dignity of your persecutor even when he or she is not respecting yours?

For the Children

What does it mean to be "persecuted?"

A long time ago, when the Church was brand-new, people were so afraid of Christians that they tried to kill everyone who followed Christ. But why? What were they so afraid of?

Here's the thing—what Jesus asks us to do is exactly the opposite of what the world thinks we should do. Think about all the advertisements and game shows on TV. We're supposed to have the newest and coolest toys, wear the best clothes, be the most beautiful, the most famous, have the most money or friends. We're supposed to be trying to beat everyone else.

But that doesn't make us happy. Jesus gives us a very different idea of living. He says give everything away and follow him. He says the last shall be first and the first shall be last. He says if we want to lead, we have to be a servant. And he didn't just say all this—he showed us by the way he lived.

Why would this make us happy? Because God created us in his image. This doesn't have anything to do with how we look. It means that our souls were made to love, just like God loves, and we will be happiest when we are living out God's plan for us.

We use our bodies—in other words, our actions—to show that love to him. That also means showing love to people we meet, because they are made in God's image, just like we are. But as long as we go chasing after things instead of God, we'll never be happy. We'll just get bored and want something new or different.

Jesus told his disciples, "If the world hates you, realize that it hated me first. If you belonged to the world, the world would love its own; but because you do not belong to the world, and I have chosen you out of the world, the world hates you." (John 15:18–19)

You see? Jesus chose us out of the world. Chasing after things that are new or different—things that don't last—is how the world works. And if we live differently, some people aren't going to like it.

It's been 2,000 years since Jesus died and rose from the dead. Christianity has taken over the world, and hardly anybody would try to kill you for following Christ now. But that doesn't mean you won't be persecuted. It's just going to look a little different now. Some day, someone is going to make fun of you because you believe in Jesus. He might call you names. He might try to make you do something you know is wrong, because if you betray Jesus, it will make him feel better about not following or believing in him himself.

Persecution is no fun, but if you can stay faithful through those times, your love for God and your trust in him will be stronger because of it. That's why Jesus says those who are persecuted because of him are blessed—because it brings them closer to him!

Just Live It

Can you think of a time when someone made fun of you for doing something Jesus said to do? How did it make you feel? Silly? Embarrassed? What did you say? What did you do? Say a prayer for that person right now. Then ask God to teach you what to say or what to do the next time it happens.

Chapter 9

"Rejoice and be glad, for your reward will be great in heaven" (Matthew 5:12).

Putting It All Together: Faith in the Modern World

We ended the last chapter with an acknowledgment that authentic Christian living is inherently threatening to the nonbeliever and the lukewarm believer alike. We must be prepared for pushback. We must be ready to defend the faith by word and by example.

But this isn't a license to go around throwing rosaries and holy cards at everyone we meet.

Our job is to evangelize the world by our lives, not by displaying holy externals or even by bringing faith overtly into every conversation. True faith expresses itself in quiet actions that rarely need religious commentary attached to them.

So what does that mean, exactly? What does it take to be a disciple of Christ in today's world? What are those quiet actions that do their own evangelizing?

No one can answer that question for anyone else. But this much I know: a living faith walks a fine line between conflicting world views (for example, when politics is involved). "Enter through the narrow gate; for the gate is wide and the road broad that leads to destruction, and those who enter through it are many. How narrow the gate and constricted the road that leads to life. And those who find it are few" (Matthew 7:13–14).

The gospel puts us at odds with all human philosophies, liberal and conservative alike. Institutional solutions, whether in the Church or the political arena, don't replace our responsibility. We can't wait for some conglomerate entity to do God's work for us. When we are confronted personally with the many problems of a fallen world, how are we to respond?

What is our personal responsibility as a Christian, for instance, to the people who hold signs at highway off-ramps? To poor families in our children's schools? How do we weigh our response against poor choices made by those adults—drug or alcohol abuse, and so on? Do those considerations lessen our duty to them in any way? How are we to treat those who do things our faith tells us is wrong: sexual behaviors, providing for abortions, playing fast and loose with the truth to get ahead?

All these are questions we have to wrestle with. It's far too easy for the problems of the world to get shoved down the priority list by the stuff of everyday life. But even within that ordinary life, dulled by routine and repetition, we must witness to a higher law. We have to follow Jesus' example and call the world to become a better version of itself.

At the same time, we have to be careful how that manifests in our attitudes and actions. Righteousness and self-righteousness are only a hair's breadth apart; it's hard to separate judging people's actions from judging the people themselves. Perhaps the best place to begin is to err on the side of grace: "Do to others whatever you would have them do to you." (Matthew 7:12) Interestingly, those words are Jesus' preface to the above admonition about the narrow path. Reading these verses together reminds us that our primary business is to mind our own spiritual journey, not try to judge others'.

Each of us is called to serve in unique ways; each of us has gifts and contributions to make that no one else can make, purposes for which God put us on the earth. Perhaps you are called to serve the homeless by supporting a shelter, and I am called to give money or food directly to those begging beside the road, while our neighbor is called to live among the homeless via a Catholic Worker house. Maybe it's not so much about performing the right action as it is simply about acting.

In the modern world, religion is often maligned as mindless superstition, as a closed-minded rigidity in which the believer thinks he or she has it all figured out. Unfortunately, all too many who claim the Christian faith perpetuate this view; as G.K. Chesterton noted, it's not that Christianity has been tried and found wanting, but that it's so difficult, it hasn't been tried at all.

Discipleship is a constant search for deeper understanding of God and God's will in our lives. Such a process never, ever involves having all the answers. That's an uncomfortable reality; as humans, we like to have the world wrapped up in neat, tidy boxes that don't require discernment. But being a lifelong seeker means we're never satisfied with the *status quo*. We have to be constantly looking in the mirror at our own faults and imposing action on ourselves to become better reflections of the God in whose image we are made. There's very little room in that paradigm for worrying about other people's actions. We have plenty of work before us just to deal with our own.

It's time to live deliberately, to walk thoughtfully through the minefield of real-life moral dilemmas. It's time our faith stops being something we do on Sundays and special occasions and becomes something that informs every decision we make, however minor. It's time to turn all of life into a prayer—not a pious, ivory-tower kind of prayer, but prayer in the sense that we place ourselves in God's presence and turn to him for his input again and again through the day. I guarantee, if we all do this, the world will be a very different place.

We don't have to wear Catholicism like a designer garment that must always be remarked upon. If faith is integrated into our lives, everyone around us will recognize us as Christians, whether or not we talk about it. And if we live a peaceful, joy-filled (that is to say, not confrontational or bitter or angry) life, regardless of suffering or meekness or humbling circumstances or persecution, it will attract people...and sometimes repel...and sometimes, invite persecution.

Rejoice and be glad, for your reward will be great in heaven.

For the Children

What does God want me to do with my life?

That is a big question, and nobody can answer it for you. God has a plan for you. It may be getting married and having kids. It may be the priesthood or religious life. But the only way you'll know God's big plan for your life is to start listening to the little ones—the ones happening every day, one moment at a time.

Every day, you have choices to make. You might see someone being bullied. How are you supposed to respond? Stand up to the bully or go get a teacher?

You might see that someone left a mess of fast-food wrappers on the ground by your car at the store. Can you go get a trash bag and throw it away before it pollutes God's earth?

You might feel bad because someone is being mean to you. Should you tell on them, talk directly to them, or just ignore it?

Sometimes the answer is obvious. Other times there may be several good answers—or no good answer at all. But every choice we make brings us closer to Jesus or further away from him. If we want to be disciples of Christ, we have to live as if he's walking right next to us. Then, every time we run into a situation we don't know how to handle, we can just turn to him and ask for help. It may take some time, but we can learn to hear his voice.

It's really easy to see other people's faults, but it's more important for us to see our own and be willing to change so that we become more like Jesus. Being a disciple of Christ means we're always trying to follow him better. Not just on Sundays, not just during religion class, but all the time—when we're playing with friends, when we're doing chores at home...always. Every moment of every day, we should be trying to live out the beatitudes—being humble, trusting God even when it hurts, showing mercy, being clean of heart, making peace.

If we do that, people will recognize that we are Christians. Then we don't have to talk to people to share our faith. Our actions will do it for us. Sometimes that will mean people will persecute us.

Rejoice and be glad, Jesus says, for your reward will be great in heaven.

Just Live It: Parting Thoughts

What are the habitual practices and actions in my life that make my faith in Christ visible to the world—something more substantial than wearing a cross around my neck? What about my practice of faith is at odds with the world? Where is my line in the sand? What habits and behaviors must I not tolerate in myself if I want to follow Christ? What is God calling me specifically to do, whether or not anyone else is called to the same? How can I focus more on my call to action and less on everyone else's?

Finally, here's a question to ask many times every day:

Lord, what is your will for me today, in this situation?

PATTERN 1

The pattern on this page relates to the project on page 30.

PATTERN 2

The pattern on this page relates to the project on page 30.

Joy to the World:
Advent Activities for Your Family

ISBN: 978-0-7648-1937-7

Here's a treasure trove of exciting ideas that will enable your family to focus anew on preparing for the holy time of Advent and Christmas! With a fresh, lively set of suggestions, *Joy to the World* will help lay the foundation for long-lasting family memories:

• The **Advent calendar**, where daily activities are organized into four categories of Service, Spiritual Growth, "Homebody," and Pure Fun.

• The **Evening Ritual**, which incorporates the Advent wreath and the Jesse tree and features simplified Scriptures that young children can readily understand.

• The "**Good Deeds Manger**," which puts the family's focus on preparing their hearts for the coming of Christ.

Bring Lent to Life:
Activities and Reflections for Your Family

ISBN: 978-0-7648-2004-5

Don't just give something up for Lent! Gather your family, and with Kate Basi's fresh ideas, you will *Bring Lent to Life*! Fasting is not just giving up candy, almsgiving is more than giving away your unused allowance, and prayer becomes active. Embark on the adventure of practicing the three tenets of Lent in new ways:

• The **Easter Tree** grows with symbols (nails, an empty egg, three dimes, and more) rooted in Scripture and blooms with flowers through your Lenten observance.

• **Sunday Love Letters** (and drawings) share the love of Christ with family members.

• Crafts, family outings, recipes, and other activities help reveal the meaning of Lent.

To Order Visit Your Local Bookstore
Call 800-325-9521 • Visit liguori.org